The Story of
Mazawattee Tea

John Boon Densham
1814-1886
Founder of the firm Densham & Sons Tea Merchants.

The Story of Mazawattee Tea

Diana James

The Pentland Press Limited
Edinburgh Cambridge Durham USA

First published in 1996
by The Pentland Press Limited
1 Hutton Close,
South Church,
Bishop Auckland,
Durham.

ISBN : 1 85821 453 X

Typeset and printed by
Lintons Printers, Crook, County Durham.

*In fond Memory of
Marion Densham*

FOREWORD

My memories of the Mazawattee Head Office are those of a child in the Thirties. It meant nothing to me that Great Grandfather had founded the firm in the mid 1860s, or that the once famous business empire was now beginning to crumble, weighed down by financial troubles and soon to vanish beneath the fire bombs of the 1940 London blitz.

Tower Hill in those days was, in itself, a vital part of the old City. Most of the vans from the various tea wharves were horse drawn and the streets were cobbled. I can still see - and hear - the huge dray horses as they struggled for grip, often striking sparks with their hooves. Most would stop for a long, well earned drink from the horse troughs at the end of the climb.

As you approached from the monument early in the morning, the Billingsgate Fish Market spilled onto the pavement and the bustling porters, their flat, hard hats piled with boxes of gleaming fish, performed incredible feats of balancing - accompanied by language that had to be heard to be believed!

The Mazawattee office and the bonded warehouse formed the goal as you gained the top of Tower Hill, the name painted in gold letters pointing in several directions so that no visiting tourist could miss the imposing building. During the day, in the big open space above the Tower of London, food stalls were set up, sword swallowers and amateur actors performed and pick-pockets lurked, while Donald Soper (now Lord) preached peace and love to the lunch time crowds.

What is not generally known is that Mazawattee was parent company of many fading enterprises. The brightly polished brass plate on the front of the building had inscribed on it such names as:

Densham & Sons Ltd - the loose leaf tea as opposed to the packet trade - also the coffee (Dee & Ess) side.

Samuel Allen & Co. Ltd - confectionery and chocolates.

The Decorated Tin Plate Co. Ltd - Pioneers in colour printing on tins. All pre-war Yardley's powder tins, with sprinkler tops, were made at the New Cross factory. The workmanship was beautiful, as the wide range of Mazawattee tins shows.

Lorimer - Marshall Ltd - Wholesale chemists who produced "Bay Rum" hair tonic, spices and flavourings for cakes.

At the great front door my mother and I would be ushered in by a beribboned commissionaire, the smiling Mr Crane, resplendent in the Mazawattee livery of khaki and red. He would whisk us up to the Chairman's Office, a large, bright room with panoramic views of the Tower and the busy waterway of the River Thames.

In the 1930s the third generation to occupy the Chair was my uncle, Joseph Alexander Densham, who would let me prowl around looking at the company's trophies. On the wall hung the original oil painting of *The Old Folks At Home*, a granny and little girl, whose beatific smiles and raised cups had become the famous trade mark. There were other strikingly colourful advertisements, including *The Jolly Boys* - three happy young negroes, forever enjoying their favourite Mazawattee tea. Perhaps the most prized possession was a glass box of the Gartmore Estate *Golden Tips*, with a purchase document dated 7 May 1891 when, amid wild excitement in the Mincing Lane auction rooms, Mazawattee paid £25 10s per lb for the finest Ceylon tea leaves. Also framed was another record breaker - an identical cheque, for what in those days would have been a king's ransom, the exact amount being £85,802 8s 8d - signed by John Lane Densham. This was the largest sum by many thousands ever paid in one amount for tea duty to Customs and Excise.

All these vanished amid a hail of bombs in the last war and Mazawattee Tea, once a name to conjure with, is now just a memory.

Acknowledgements

Thanks are due to Anne and Jeremy Pemberton for the attractive front cover and to my son, Stephen, for his constant support. This, too, applies to the Densham family for whom this book is written. Company reports, culled from *The Grocer*, have been of immense help, as have my Grandfather's private letters and my Aunt Evie Tryon's diaries. So too have the late Revd. Costin Densham's memories and those of Sylvia Lambert, now Mrs Hodge, while Senior Engineer Robert McGreivy gave me a brilliant insight into the layout and workings of the New Cross factory. It was he who installed the first tea bag machine in the country. P A Hebdon's long term interest has been much appreciated and during my research very many kind people have sent me valuable information about the company and fascinating bits of memorabilia for my Mazawattee collection. Indeed, too many to mention all by name but I am truly grateful to them. Last, but by no means least, special thanks to my husband Harry, for finding the time in his busy life to photograph objects to be used as illustrations for

THE STORY OF MAZAWATTEE TEA

Notes

Mazawattee did not survive to the decimal currency and kilogram age so £ s d and pounds and ounces are used throughout. Sri Lanka, formerly Ceylon, is now a republic within the British Commonwealth but the name Ceylon is still in use for the tea of the country and found in our shops today.

A printer's block for the new Ceylon Tea.

List of Black and White Illustrations

In the Beginning

The story starts with a mystery. Who was Charlie Lees? Where did he come from and how did he meet the Denshams of Devonshire and enter into partnership with John Boon Densham?

Even if these questions are never answered it is certain that there was quite an important tea firm, called Lees and Densham, in existence in 1865. It appears in one of the 'Duty Paid' lists published by *The Grocer**between 1863 and 1867. For the week ending 3 October 1865 it paid on 10,121 lb. of tea. Indeed, Lees and Densham was 39th on a list of some 60 firms, with now famous names such as Ridgway and Tetley not far above them. The top firm at that time was Peek Bros., having paid duty on over 95,000 lb of tea.

John Boon Densham's early years were spent as a chemist and druggist in Plymouth. The Census return for 30 March 1851 records his age as 36 and that he lived at 55 Old Town Street, St Andrews, Plymouth. In the house, besides him and his wife Anne, were his sister, brother-in-law and three young sons, who were later to play vital parts in the as yet unborn firm, Densham and Sons. Also recorded are three assistant chemists and a servant girl. There was no mention of tea, but chemists did sell, and blend, loose leaf teas from China and India. At this time the Temperance movement was gaining momentum and many considered tea to be the perfect answer to strong liquor. Plymouth, being a thriving port, saw its full quota of drunkenness and the expression 'tee total' and 'taking the pledge' were beginning to be heard.

The Densham family were strict Baptists and may well have been influenced by what they saw. 'The cup that cheers but does not inebriate' was a splendid slogan! Previously tea had been an expensive luxury - thought to be too good for the working classes. It was locked away from the servants in elegant teapoys or caddies. However, the lowering of tea duty made it obtainable by the general public and, in Britain, tea drinking was here to stay!

In 1870, at the age of 55, John Boon began to keep a small black account book and the first entry reads:-

* A weekly trade journal

Stock taken				January 1870			
Lees & Densham	4719	14	2	Debts	7022	8	5
Dr Emmerson	500	0	0	Total Stock	1931	18	1
James Doudney	450	0	0	Fixtures	90	0	0
Char. Lees	2000	0	0	Cash in Bank	450	0	0
A Densham	25	5	7	Balance	1000	0	0
B Densham	92	6	8				
J B Densham	2707	0	1				
	£10494	**6**	**6**		**£10494**	**6**	**6**

Examined and found to be correct
J B Densham
Edw Densham
Alfred Densham
B Densham

In 1873, trading from 11 Philpot Lane in the City of London, the account book records that the firm had been reborn as Densham & Sons. The last mention of Charlie Lees was on 31 December 1873 and nothing more is known of him.

By that date profits had risen to £19, 337 9s 1d and, on a buoyant market, the firm was steadily climbing, selling loose leaf tea to be blended and packed by family grocers.

The Board was still composed of John Boon, his three elder sons, and various relations as sleeping partners but, in 1881, a new star appeared on the horizon - the youngest son, John Lane Densham, entered the scene. As a youth he had developed consumption and doctors shook their heads, giving him just a year to live. All his life he was to be dogged by poor health, suffering from stomach trouble and nervous disorder. But rather than sink down under the specialist's death sentence he decided to fight, and took off round the world. After a year he was strong enough to throw himself into the family business, serving his apprenticeship as a commercial traveller and, working on commission with 30/- and a box tricycle, he canvassed the grocers of Kent, Surrey and Sussex.

Young John Lane was one of those rare, dynamic characters with an infectious sense of humour and a generous nature that made him popular in London and with the country retailers. He had an extremely happy family life which, over the years, produced fourteen children. His father's little account book records that the firm relied more and more on him and

DENSHAM'S
MILKY JUICE OF DANDELION
AND
Densham's Dandelion Pills,
Prepared from the Milky Juice.

Indigestion, with its many distressing consequences, always proceeds from a sluggish or unhealthy state of the Liver.

The Milky Juice of the Dandelion Root is the only medicine known that produces a healthy action of that important organ; those, therefore, who suffer from Indigestion, should take Mr. Densham's preparation, which contains all the medicinal properties of the root.

The Juice is sold in Bottles, at 4s. each,
and the Pills in Bottles, at 1s. 1½d., 2s. 9d., and 4s. 6d. each.

Prepared by Mr. DENSHAM, Chemist,
At his Laboratory and Old-Established Medicine House,

55, OLD-TOWN STREET, PLYMOUTH.
Sold also by all Druggists in the Kingdom.

An advertisement for John Boon Densham's special preparation in the Plymouth Directory of 1857.

The Mazawattee Head Office on Tower Hill, about 1888.

that a great deal of the income, drawn during the 1884/87 period by the partners, came from John Lane's profits. He was still a humble traveller working on commission in 1887 and records that his share was £5,683. From 1885 he kept a daily diary, noting expenses and savings and was delighted that the tricycle obviously paid off. The following two columns show the miles he travelled and amount he saved on fares:-

Saved on Tricycle

Miles		Account		
25		£1	2	0
27	June 10		15	0
54	July 3	3	16	6
25	July 6		15	0
34	July 7	1	5	0
30	Aug 19	1	3	0
14	Sept 28		3	6

All of this amounted to an awful lot of pedalling!

The entry in John Lane's diary for Wednesday 8 December 1886 is brief and sad:-
'Dear Father's funeral'.

This was the end of an era.

The Boom Years

On the death of old John Boon the three brothers made John Lane a partner - no longer to work on commission and free to use his fertile imagination for wide publicity. He was a great believer in all forms of advertising and lost no time in putting the firm's tea dramatically before the public. It was vital to create a really snappy trade mark and he spent a day in the Guildhall library working out a name that was eye-catching and easy to remember. Finally he settled on the Hindoo word 'Mazathe', meaning luscious, and the Singhalese 'Wattee', descriptive of a garden or growth. The two words, put together, read 'Mazathawattee' but, on the advice of Davis & Davis, their printers, the 'tha' was dropped and Mazawattee Tea was born. In 1887 the trade mark was officially registered and was to become world famous. The public was fascinated by this unusual name and it spawned several cartoons. One shows a little black page, offering a silver salver displaying packets of tea. The balloon from this boy's mouth asks: 'Massa - wot tea?'

It was around this time that the delightful picture, entitled *The Old Folks At Home* was launched and became an instant favourite. It shows a smiling, bonneted and shawled grandmother and her bespectacled granddaughter, happily drinking their cups of Mazawattee tea. It was used as a series on tins, on posters and large enamelled metal advertisements and tea packets and is perhaps the only thing remembered today - when Mazawattee is sometimes recalled as Granny's tea. The original model of the granny in the oil painting was Mary Ann Clarke, wife of George Clarke, an Islington bootmaker. Young Adelaide, her granddaughter, was to sit as the little girl but she was overcome with shyness and her place was taken by the child next door, Alice Emma Nichols.* Alice Emma wears a dainty mob cap and appears to have a Paisley pattern dress in the same design as the table cloth. The artist is unknown but seems to have taken trouble in providing an attractive scene with a table set with antique china and a fine silver spoon with sugar basin and tongs - but no teapot.+

* Information supplied by the writer and collector, Paul Antony Hebdon, who is Alice Emma Nichols's grandson.

+ Several sitters were used by advertisement artists and A. J. Elsley often employed Mary Pegg, whose attractive old face features on an early calendar, entitled *Mazawattee Grandma.*

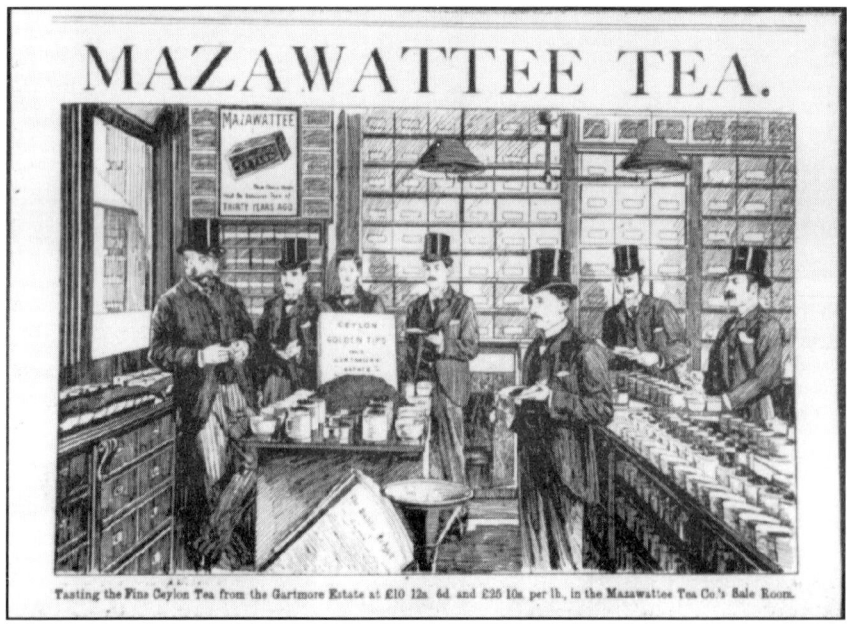

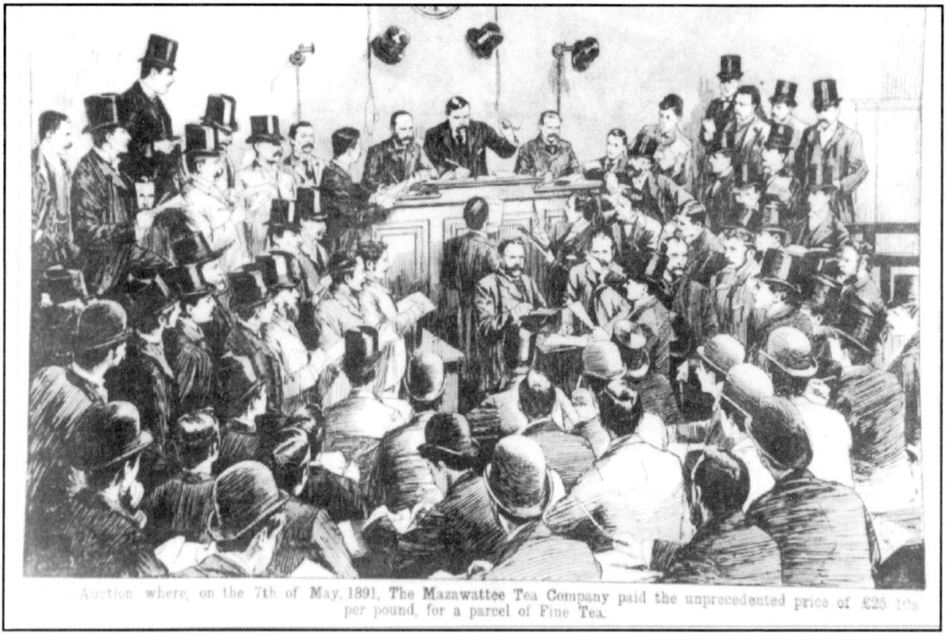
Auction where, on the 7th of May, 1891, The Mazawattee Tea Company paid the unprecedented price of £25 10s per pound, for a parcel of Fine Tea.

The public auction of the first Golden Tips Ceylon tea leaves. Mazawattee paid £25 10s. Just in front of the auctioneer Alexander Jackson can be seen, hands raised, making the winning bid.

MAZAWATTEE TEA.
MAZAWATTEE
THIRTY YEARS AGO
CEYLON
GOLDEN TIPS
Tasting the Fine Ceylon Tea from the Gartmore Estate at £10 12s 6d and £25 10s per lb., in the Mazawattee Tea Co.'s Sale Room.

Tasting the tea in the Mazawattee sale room.

An advertisement for Dee & Ess (Densham & Sons) Zamor coffee in a 1914 diary.
The opposite page shows the Mazawattee offices on Tower Hill.

One of the Blending Rooms at Tower Hill.

Still pedalling furiously around the country John Lane celebrated his promotion by selling his box tricycle for £11 5s 0d and buying a safety bicycle. He was pleased with the good return he had achieved, for after riding 387 miles, he reckoned he had saved £14 13s 0d on rail fares.

From the mid-nineteenth century public advertising was greatly increased by the production of large enamelled iron signs, and Mazawattee was one of the first companies to appreciate the potential advantages of this form of publicity.

A long term contract with the affluent railways ensured the appearance of eye-catching advertisements for Mazawattee Tea on every railway platform in the British Isles. A cartoon of the day depicts a distraught old lady, having missed her destination, bitterly complaining to a porter that every station was either called *Gentlemen* or *Mazawattee*!

A Victorian cartoon. (Courtesy, Antony Hebdon).

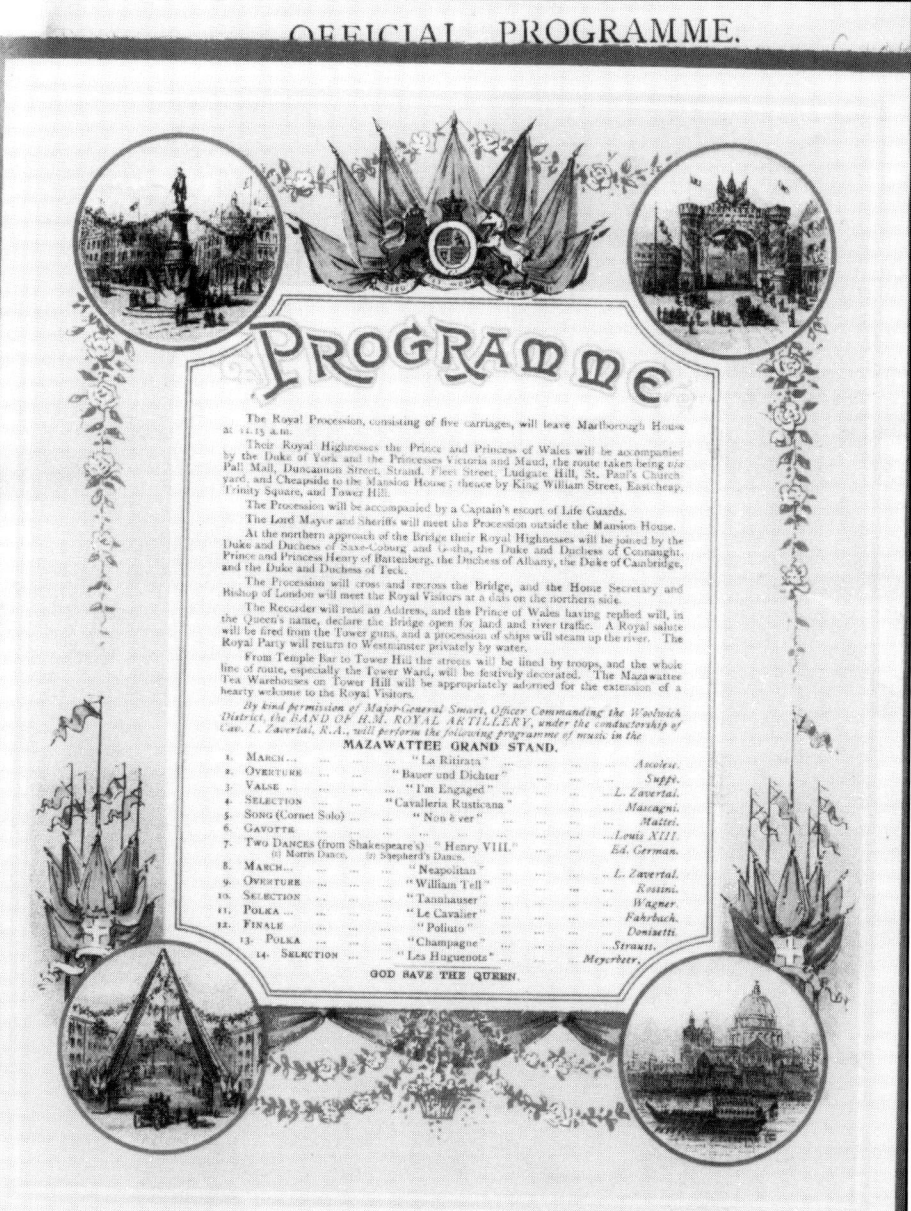

Official Programme for the opening of Tower Bridge, 30 June 1894.

The Mazawattee Grand Stand for the opening of Tower Bridge, 30 June 1894.

What Price Ceylon?

On 28 October 1878 Ceylon tea first made its mark in the London market. It possessed a fresh new flavour and Mazawattee identified itself with it, for a while even incorporating the name Ceylon with its own trade name. Ceylon madness gripped the tea trade and in order to stay at the top it was imperative to keep the firm's image before the public. Hence, what the newspapers called The Great Tea War began.

The finest quality Ceylon tea was known as "Golden Tips", which were young leaf buds, hand sorted, possessing a rich, flowery flavour hitherto untasted and consequently fantastically expensive. Bidding went wild as firms pushed the price higher and higher. On 10 March 1891 Mazawattee - amid a round of cheering and waving of hats in the Mincing Lane Auction Rooms - trumped rival bids with one of £25 10s per pound, intending it to be the centre-piece for their stand in the Great Chicago Exhibition of 1893. Sixty thousand people visited the picturesque Ceylon Court in the World's Colombian Exposition. Here, 4,596,490 cups of tea were served by Singhalese in flowing robes, and 1,161,624 packets of prime quality leaves were sold.

These were stirring times and big changes were taking place in the tea trade, when fortunes could be made - and lost - in the great boom years. Steam was on the horizon, but it was still the age of the famous tea clippers, when ships loaded up at Foochow with new seasons "First Chop"* leaves from the estates in May or June. Then the rush was on and the fast, specially designed vessels spread their vast canvas sails and made a dash for home. The Suez Canal did not open until November 1869, so they had to take the long route around the Cape of Good Hope, always anxious that the tiers of tea chests should not shift; that they should stay dry and the tender new leaves fresh and sweet. Fighting through monsoons, typhoons and the terrible storms of the Bay of Biscay they hoped to arrive early in a British port so that the Captain and crew could collect the fat bonus promised for a speedy passage. The glamour and romance of these magical clipper ships caught the public imagination and the most exciting race took place in 1866.

Eleven magnificent clipper ships set sail from Foochow, over 400 miles north of the Canton estuary, making all possible speed in a dash back to an English port. Fully loaded, they spread their vast canvas sails on 28

*The first tender leaves to be plucked from the bushes took place in 1866.

A Densham Family Group. Taken in the autumn of 1896 in their mansion in Croydon, Surrey.
The author's mother is the tall girl on the right of her father, John Lane Densham.

A LONDON TEA GARDEN OF 100 YEARS AGO.
(FROM A DRAWING BY GEORGE MORLAND.)

This advertisement appeared in The Graphic, 21 April 1894.

May. On 28 August it was reported from the Azores that four of the fastest were dead level. Excitement mounted in England and many bets were laid as telegrams back to Mincing Lane reported the progress of the leaders - each carrying a cargo of some million pounds of leaf tea. In the English Channel the contest was finally between the *Ariel* and the *Taeping*. At that stage the owners of the two ships agreed that the race was a dead heat and to divide the 10s per ton premium that the winner would have been able to claim - though many bitterly grumbled that *Ariel* had the edge on her rival. However, both triumphantly completed the voyage on the 6 September, the other clippers docking not long after.

Sadly these beautiful vessels vanished with the age of steam though, to begin with, it was thought that all the metal used in the ship would impair the flavour of the tea. Most of the clippers have gone, but luckily one still remains. The famous *Cutty Sark* is on view to the public in a dry dock alongside the Thames at Greenwich. She was launched in 1869 and would have been able to carry up to 1,200,000 lbs of tea. It is also memorable as being the ship that brought over the famous Gartmore 'Golden Tips'. Mazawattee salesman were given small phials of the leaves to interest their customers.

Densham and Sons handled the loose leaf trade and never had great dealings with China for, by 1870, imports to the UK of Indian tea topped the 15 million mark. In 1879 the sale of China tea had reached its peak and from then on steadily declined. This was partly because the Indian producers were willing to make up small consignments of fresh leaves and dispatch them straight off to the European market. The Chinese growers dropped behind trying to ship off large quantities at one time. Hence a certain staleness was noticed as the leaves had been left in the warehouses until a full complement was made up.

Gargantuan tea duty cheques were at this time exploited as advertising material. *The Daily Mail* of 4 May 1898 ran a column:

The Fierce Tea Fight

The Mazawattee people have just paid the biggest cheque ever for tea duty and are not too proud to mention the fact. They have filled the town with reverberant announcements about it and pictorial representations of the cheque confront one everywhere. If you get into a hansom you find a cheque for £63,147 2s 10d lying on your seat; if you ride in a bus, tram or penny steam boat, the sum of £63,147 haunts your gaze and will presumably do so until another tea man will arise and raise the Mazawattee cheque an additional ten or twenty thousand.

A *Daily Mail* representative questioned Mr R A McQuitty, a director of the Mazawattee Company, on this subject yesterday:

"We hold the three records in the trade. We have paid a cheque for duty £2,500 larger in amount than any cheque ever paid in the Customs; we have bought tea at £26 15s the pound, the highest price on record, and our brokers, Messrs Gow, Wilson and Stanton, have purchased on our behalf over 10,000 chests in one 'break' which is the largest in the world's history."

What's in a packet?

On the home market many dealers were beginning to feel uneasy, or green tea was falling out of favour and some doctors declared it bad for nerves and digestion. To make it look more appetising, unscrupulous traders added Prussian Blue - or even deadly verdigris - to disguise the natural greyish colour and turn it a delightfully bright green. The public understandably became rattled and to allay generally concern, Densham & Sons hurriedly attached a chemist's analytical report to their two best quality teas, assuring customers that the purity of the unadulterated leaves would not only enhance the delicate flavour but soothe the most irritable digestion.

Out of this worry came a great step forward, intended to counter the problem of the additives in loose tea. Packaging was introduced. After a slow start due to the reluctance of the grocers and dealers, it began to revolutionise the market. Previously, tea had been supplied in chests and half chests to wholesalers and family grocers who would sell it 'straight', or blended to suit the customer's wishes, and grocers could hope for a larger profit than would be earned by selling pre-weighed and pre-packed tea.

Densham & Sons eagerly leaped into the packaging trade and was amongst the first to buy suitable machinery and supply shop shelves with attractive 1lb and ¼lb packets.

In the early days the packets were in lead - then very cheap - and your ¼lb bought you just about 2¾oz of tea and 1¼oz of lead.

There was a strong Puritanical streak in the Densham family and John Lane put it into practice in his business activities. He appeared before a select committee in the House of Commons and is alleged to have said that 'a false balance is an abomination in the sight of the Lord'. Be that as it may, he was partly responsible for getting the net weight law changed in Great Britain.

In 1895 Densham & Sons (the Parent Company) was trading from Ceylon House, 49 & 51 Eastcheap, selling loose leaf tea, but the Mazawattee Ceylon Tea Company was flying high and had moved into a huge building, complete with its own warehouse and deep vaults, on the top of Tower Hill.

In 1864 this ground had been in the care of the Royal Hospital of St. Katherine's-by-the-Tower, but the Trustees had leased the whole site to George Myers, a speculative builder, on an 84 years building lease, expiring in 1948. The building erected by Myers was of massive proportions and he encased in brick the largest cubic space he could, for in those days there was no limit on height. The resulting monster was bitterly regretted by the clergy of All Hallows Barking-by-the-Tower, who grumbled that it cut off the light, air and views, not only from the old church but also the neighbouring streets. For Mazawattee, however, this accommodation gave plenty of room for the China, Indian and Ceylon sales counters with blending machines that could guzzle a ton of leaves a a time, advertising department, packing, tea-tasting and general offices.

Apart from being ideal for conducting business, this huge complex was perfect for entertaining visitors and viewing great occasions. One such was the opening of Tower Bridge on 30 June 1894. The whole building was bedecked with brightly coloured flags and embellished with floral garlands and patriotic greetings to Edward, Prince of Wales and Princess Alexandra. The Royal Procession consisted of five carriages of Queen Victoria's family, including royalty from Europe. It was accompanied by the magnificent turn-out of a Captain's escort of the Life Guards while the Band of the Royal Artillery played rousing music beneath the Mazawattee grandstand. And what a grandstand it turned out to be! Every window was crammed with cheering members of the staff and their families and a sumptuous buffet luncheon - no doubt with tea provided for the ladies - was served after the official opening. The great building was used for many more joyful occasions, especially on Lord Mayor's Show day which always provided a reason for celebration. The Mazawattee offices and warehouse were profusely decorated with huge flags floating from the upper windows and vari-coloured banners carried from the roof to the street. Members of the grocery trade and their families were given seats at the windows and 'Messrs Alfred, Edward, Benjamin and John Lane Densham were untiring in their efforts to promote the comfort of their guests'.*

After the procession had passed a champagne luncheon was always served. Again tea was provided for the ladies!

The great success of the brothers was looked upon with jaundiced eyes by some jealous rivals and in July 1889 Densham & Sons took Dobie McCabe & Co to court over a matter of tea wrappers. Mr Hardy QC, in opening the case for the plaintiffs, said that the name - The Mazawattee Co - had been in use since 1887. Large sums of money had been spent on advertising. The defendants, Dobie, McCabe, had started marketing

---

* *The Grocer* - 16 November 1889

packet tea labelled Mallewattee Tea Co. They had applied to have this trade name registered, but the application had not been granted. The design of the defendant's packets had, in his opinion, been deliberately adopted for the purpose of passing off their goods as the goods of the plaintiffs.

It turned out to be a long and interesting case, enlivened by legal sparring. In his final summing up, * Mr Justice North declared:

'This, therefore, was a case in which the defendants had deliberately copied and it was clear that they were not so scrupulous as to refrain from copying the mark of another person... The injunction would therefore go in the terms asked by the writ, and as a matter of course, with costs.'

Every business had its sharks and confidence tricksters. In January 1895, Densham & Sons was taken to court by one Arthur Henry Deakin, managing director of the Marza Manufacturing Company. He claimed to have invented the word Marza as a trade mark for various articles. This was opposed by the respondents on the grounds that their tea was known by that name. The applicant started proceedings to get the Mazawattee mark expunged from the register. Early in 1895, in the Chancery Division, the case was heard before Lords Justices Lindley, Lopes and Kay.

Teams of legal experts were fielded by both sides with a phalanx of back-up witnesses. The case lasted three days and concluded with the dismissal of the appeal of the Marza trade mark with costs.

In Lord Justice Lindley's summing up he said:

'I confess I thought when this appeal was opened that it was about as hopeless a one as I have ever heard, and I think so still.'

In his private diary John Lane records the fee for his Q.C.: 'Sir R E Webster £52 10s.'+

To mark winning the case he sent a "Thank offering to the Consumption Hospital" and noted, "A red letter day both natural and spiritual."

---

* A full account can be read in *The Grocer*, July 1889.

+ Full report in *The Grocer*, 4 May 1898.

Small gift box for a roundel of chocolate commemorating the coronation of Edward VII.

The New Cross Complex, 1901.

The Jolly Boys. An early tin when tea was 3lbs for 5/6.

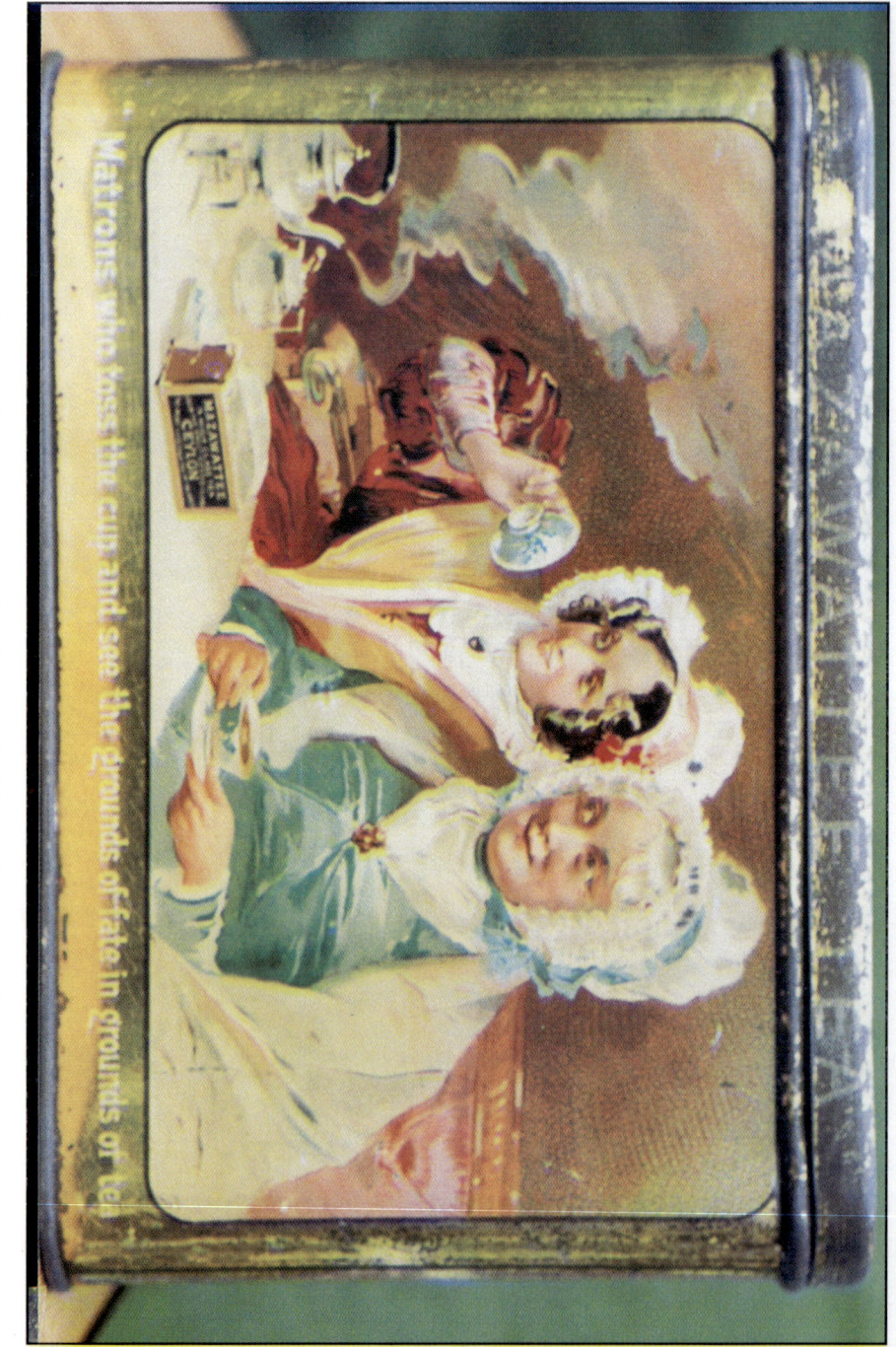

Matrons that toss the cup and see the grounds of fate in the grounds of tea.

Britannia's welcome to Mazawattee cocoa. October 1901. A colourful tin tray with a reduced reproduction of the poster taken from an oil painting by the Victorian artist Maynard Brown.

Richard Densham and his cousin, the Author, admire part of her collection. (Courtesy of Anne Densham)

A patriot tea tin showing the allies, in the First World War.

Louis Wain's Cats' Ball

Louis Wain was much in demand to do eye catching advertisements. Mazawattee commissioned several of his paintings.

Queen Mary and the young Prince of Wales. Tins showing royal portraits were much in demand.

"MAZAWATTEE GRANDMA" Artist A. J. Elsley.
Mary Pegg the grandma.

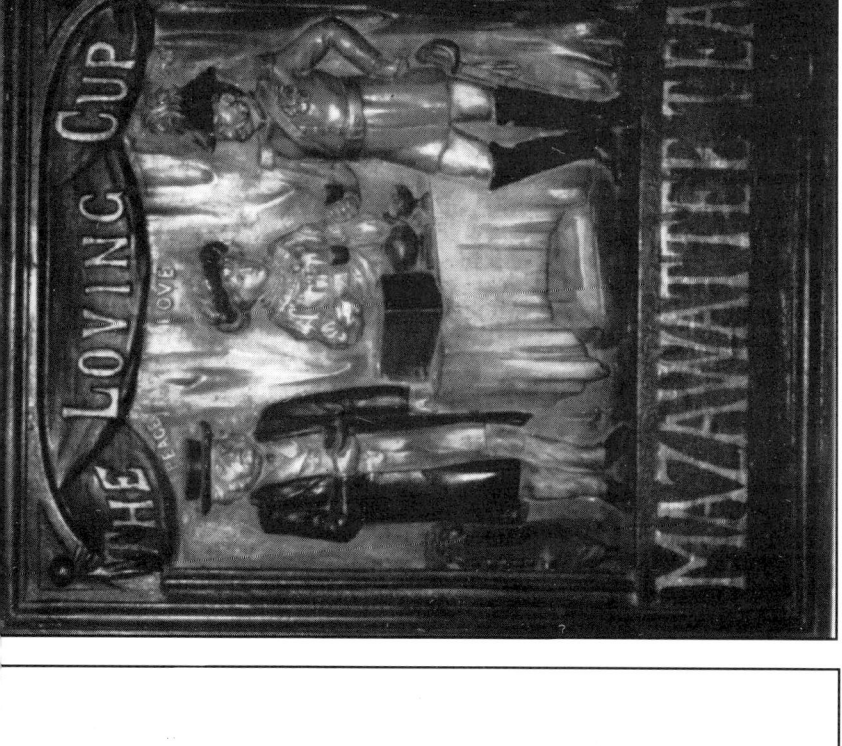

The Loving Cup. An unusual plaster model for shop display (Courtesy, Geoffrey Silverman).

A cartoon at the time of the Russian Coronation, 1895.

Now a Company

In May 1896 the business became a public company with Benjamin and John Lane as managing directors. In August 1896 a contract was drawn up so that the two elder brothers could retire and take back seats. *
It was agreed that the sum of £30,000 each to be paid to Messrs Benjamin and John Lane Densham by the said Alfred and Edward Densham in addition to their one fourth shares, such two sums of £30,000 to be paid two thirds in cash and one third in Preference and ordinary shares rateably

It was not long before John Lane became chairman of the new company.

After the great excitement of the 'Golden Tips' purchase, which had been a nine day wonder, came the battle of the mammoth cheques. In John Lane's diary for Wednesday 27 April 1898 is a triumphant entry:

'Payment of Custom's cheque £63,147 2s 10d.'

The Sun newspaper for Friday 13 May 1898 carried this report:

Mazawattee v Liptons
The fight in the tea trade and its prospects.

The tea trade joins with the general public in watching with increased interest as the days go on what card Liptons intend to play against the latest trump put down by the Mazawattee company. The Mazawattee big cheque was roughly £14,000 above Lipton's record figure.

It is understood that Liptons are making preparations to cap this with a still larger cheque, and we have the best reason to believe that large though the Lipton's cheque may be, the Mazawattee people intend to do one better. At present the field is simply divided between the Mazawattee company and Liptons, with Mazawattee just now leading.

The tea boom years were not to be repeated and John Lane's diary of February 1899 records:

'Great rise in the price of tea. At the top of April no Assam under 8½ Ceylon 8¼ China 7¼'

* Edward Densham's son, George, and Benjamin's son, Sidney, followed their fathers into the company for a while.

Still the price rose and Budget days caused constant worry with the heavy tea duty imposed by the Chancellor of the Exchequer. The threat of further increases in tea duty, strikes, political troubles at home and abroad, were all taking their physical toll. John Lane Densham still travelled the world and he was usually accompanied by his wife and older children, but ominous jottings in the diary mentioned bad stomach pains and jagged nerves. By the turn of the century he had already visited fifty-four main offices and thirty-six capital cities in the course of business. *He was interviewing representatives, solving problems, trouble-shooting and visiting tea estates in India and Ceylon. Care was taken in nurturing the company's agents - especially in South Africa where Mazawattee had a virtual monopoly. He was a well-known figure in the City of London and other companies tried to tempt him away with lucrative offers. He was asked to dine with Mr E J Hockley and to be a director of Schweppes. He noted in his private diary:

'Had a sweet feeling that I would rather sink in our own business of God's will than swim in any other way as ours is a business that is carried on by prayer. Feel that millions in money would be no temptation to me.'

Schweppes was not the only firm interested in him and he was promised a title if he gave a large sum of money and worked for a certain organisation. However, this was not a thing of which his strict Baptist conscience could approve and the suggestion was promptly turned down.

* *At this stage the Mazawattee Tea Company Ltd had offices at:*
Tower Hill, EC
Corn Exchange, Manchester
The Grocery, Liverpool
45 Newhall Street, Birmingham
2 Queen Street, Fort, Colombo
38 The Strand, Calcutta
And agencies World wide

By 1929 the company also ran offices in:
33 Temple Street, Bristol
45 Fleet Street, Dublin
16 Carlton Place, Glasgow
4-6 White Street, New York

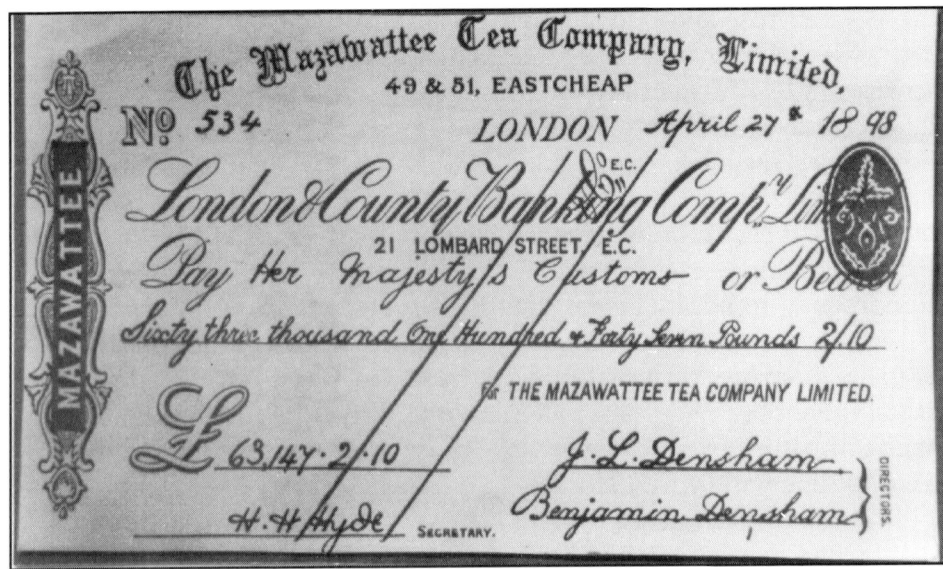

The famous Customs duty cheque of 1898.

Joseph Alexander Densham, 1883-1960.
Last chairman of the Mazawattee Tea Company.

A Fresh Venture...

On Sunday 9 September 1901 Joseph Alexander Densham celebrated his 17th birthday and the next day he joined the staff of Mazawattee, earning 6/- a week. He was John Lane's eldest son and represented the third generation of Denshams in the tea trade.

Despite hard work in all departments sales dropped at home and the crippling tea duty bankrupted many struggling firms. At Mazawattee the Board of Directors was anxious that the company should diversify and it was decided to branch out into the cocoa and chocolate trade. Vast new premises were built south of the Thames, just beside a network of railways, known as The New Cross Triangle, and the work was put into the hands of Messrs Stott & Sons of Manchester. The outlay was many thousands of pounds and the result impressive.

After an inaugural luncheon on 1 October 1901 the gentlemen of the Press were full of praise.

The Morning Leader, 2 October 1901 reported:

The Cocoa Room - How Mazawattee of Tea fame means business

The proposal of the famous Mazawattee Tea Company of £85,000 customs cheque fame, to enter upon the manufacture of cocoa and chocolate had already been recorded. Yesterday the Press were duly taken over the factory, where the new venture (and the old) are in the future to be carried on. The building resembles a big colony. Its bright brick buildings extend over many acres, and embrace a factory wall of 700 feet, and a floor space of hundreds of thousands of square feet. They are flanked by a private wharf, surrounded by railways and surmounted by a huge circular chimney 150 feet in height, which flashed out, in gigantic letters to the men of Deptford and New Cross the far from strange device "Mazawattee".

The machinery alone - the roasters, winnowers, grinders, hydraulic processors and pulveriser - are a liberal education in mechanical science. In one great lofty spacious apartment the rough beans advance through successive stages right up to the breakfast table stage. One moves through mighty stacks of tea ranged on either side like the massed waves of the Red Sea. One's lungs struggle with the overwhelming scent of pure chocolate, and one's eyes rest with relief on what looks like half the population of Lewisham manipulating the confectionery in the sweetest of taking costumes. The Mazawattee firm is making a bold bid for the cocoa and chocolate trade in this country.

Pall Mall Gazette, October 1901 had this to say:
> Nearly two thousand work people are employed, and the appearance of the rows of happy and healthily looking factory girls, clad in a becoming uniform of khaki and red, with caps plainly copied from the Irish Guards, show that the work is done under the most sanitary conditions.

As late as the 1930s Robert McGreivy, a senior engineer, remembers:
> 'The first striking thing about the factory was its construction, being so far ahead of its time. The engine room and boiler house was at the south end of the building - about 200 yards from the main entrance. This housed the weighbridge where the laden horse-drawn coal carts were check-weighed before delivering the coal to the boiler house. They then had to return to the weighbridge to be weighed for the tare. * The adjacent building to the boiler house was the engine room with its Crossley gas engine as back-up for either a bigger demand or to be used while the gas engine was being overhauled. Next again was the lead rolling mill where the lead from the Chinese tea cases was processed for re-use. The factory was almost self-supporting in that it had an Artesian well for water, a gas generator for the engine and other gas points, so the only requirement to buy was the coal for the boilers and anthracite for the gas works.

> For the most part the factory was single storey, with hollow cast iron columns supporting the roof. It was split into two corridors which ran the length of the plant from the south yard to the north yard, which was for the loading of goods, and the in and out station. Off this corridor were the separate shops for the multiple activities. Moving from the south, on the left was the specialist tea packing, which was mostly done by hand. Opposite, to the right, was the tin making and tin printing departments. Also in this room were the drying ovens for the printed flat sheets, prior

*An allowance made for the weight of the packing or wrapping around the goods.

to the cutting and forming of the finished tins. Many of our customers just wanted the printing and varnishing done and made up the tins themselves. The next shop on the left contained the tea warehouse and the assembly room for the blends, from whence these were sent to the next floor, processing through the blending drums ..... this came down to the holding bins until the packeting machinery in the next room required more raw material - there were six Roses tea packers to be kept going! Opposite, on the right, was the letter press where all the labels, for the various commodities, (and there were many) were printed and cut out. Here was also the domain of a most talented lady, The Easter Egg Queen, as we called her. Each egg was a work of art, decorated with flowers, hand spun from icing bags and so life like that it would be a shame to see them destroyed, however sumptuous. On the corridor, to the left, were the box makers who repaired or constructed boxes for further use. Their three large circular saws were kept busy all day long. Opposite them, in the days of the confectionery trade, was the Mogul Room where the chocolates were made up, coated and packaged in their fancy boxes. Left again was the loading and unloading bay and here was an extension which led to the East Wing which was the cocoa roasting, grinding and press room. This was the first process of making the chocolate for coating the centres that were formed in the Mogul Room and for the three inch diameter $\frac{1}{4}$ inch thick chocolate footballs sold to fans of the Millwall Football Club - just along Cold Blow Lane from the Mazawattee factory. They cost one penny each and the chap who sold them made them up on the morning of the home games. He was quite expert at tossing them up to the back terraces and catching the pennies coming down. The corridor, running from the south yard the whole length of the factory, had a pair of heavy wooden doors which could seal it off if required. Beyond this was what was called the New Building. This had two storeys and housed the coffee extract department. The upper floor was occupied by Lorimer Marshall, who produced a variety of food additives - such as Fluid Beef, flavourings of vanilla and lemon and banana essence. Their Lung Syrup, which was good and thick, certainly relieved a cough! The company also produced dog powders and tablets for the veterinary market. Below, on the ground floor, was the storage space for hundreds of sacks of raw coffee beans. Opposite were the coffee roasting and grinding plants. On the outside wall of the building a platform had been

A colourful tin showing scenes from 'Alice through the Looking Glass'. 1lb of tea leaves for 3/6.

A 3lb canister of Indian tea leaves.

An unusually shaped tea tin decorated with Golden Pheasants and flowering trees.

This beautiful canister was made for the Canadian market where there was a great demand for tea. It is now on show at the Kelowna Museum, British Columbia. One panel depicts a tea gatherer at work while the sides show an idyllic plantation in the mountainous region of Ceylon.

(Courtesy, Kelowna Museum)

constructed to cart the dust collecting unit from the coffee roasting. This was a cylindrical drum, about eight feet high and five foot in diameter, which had to be emptied every year. Not a pleasant job!'

And so the great New Cross works were launched and it looked as if there was a bright future in store. Many fresh jobs were created and the general public took the confectionery side to its heart - not to mention its stomach.

At the time there was no control over advertising and it was a case of dog eat dog when it came to doing down a rival in business. No important person - or occasion - was judged unfit for advertising and even royalty was used to put a product in the limelight.

Director Robert McQuitty was in charge of the advertising department and produced a series of slogans to promote the new goods.
'*Mazawattee chocolates finer than the finest French chocolate.*'
'*Mazawattee cocoa superior to any foreign chocolates.*'
'*Mazawattee milk chocolates. Vastly superior to foreign makes.*'
'*Mazawattee tea. Always the same superb quality.*'
'*Mazawattee coffee preserves intact the true oriental aromas.*'

The new cocoa was supposed to be an excellent food and widely promoted by the medical profession. An analytical report by Dr D Mackenzie MB featured in the Mazawattee diaries of the period:

> '[Mazawattee cocoa] enlivens the spirits and stimulates the mental faculties... It possesses in a remarkable degree, not merely the power of allaying thirst but also of assuaging or quenching the desire or craving for spirituous liquors. Without experimenting on myself for any such purpose, I became quite unconsciously indifferent to the use or need of spirits... This experience has been corroborated by patients and others whom I have questioned on the matter... Such a beneficial quality cannot be too extensively known.'

Launched with a flourish, the new cocoa powder was widely promoted as Mazawattee Latariba. In their DEE & ESS range Mazawattee cocoa essence was sold in 4½d tins bearing the proud boast that over 33 per cent of natural butter was used in the preparation - further, that it was produced solely by British work people. The Mazawattee coffee essence was marked in slender, long-necked bottles, priced 5½d and 10½d and christened Zamor - later to become Service Coffee. As a drink it never really caught on.

Like the tea, Mazawattee chocolates were packed in superbly decorated tins - cardboard being thought to spoil the flavour. All the containers were now made, and the artwork completed, at the New Cross factory. The firm's craftsmen were pioneers in colour printing on tin and surviving examples are now much sought after, being highly prized by present day collectors and fetch high prices. Many designs used the Art Nouveau motifs and good specimens of these, and especially ones executed by the famous cat artist, Louis Wain, are particularly in demand. Whole series were produced of nursery rhymes, royal portraits and dramatic scenes to mark special occasions. Flat tins of chocolate were sent to the Boer War soldiers in South Africa and at the coronation of Edward and Alexandra the 80,000 troops that lined the route of the two royal processions were each issued with a box of Mazawattee milk chocolates.

'Which in addition to supplying a generous quantity of highly refreshing and sustaining confection, will constitute an elegant souvenir of the historic event. The box takes the form of beautiful circular medallion tin, the lid of which bears a gold embossed representation of the King's head. Faithful as a likeness and valuable as a work of art. '*

On the face of things it appeared that this new enterprise had a glowing future but John Lane's private diary shows a troubled mind:

'*13 January 1901.* I had a great blow on hearing the result of stock-taking. The statistics of Mazawattee sales is serious, showing as it does great decrease in better packets and great increase in 1/6 ones, which do not pay.'.

'*Thursday 18 April 1901.* Feel very anxious about the Budget. Agree with Ben that if extra duty is imposed it will mean half our income gone and the business practically crippled.'

'*Sunday 24 November 1901.* We have taken a big step and I am now perfectly satisfied that if the Lord does not help us our new cocoa and chocolate business will be a partial failure and our business as a whole will be seriously crippled. Our tea business has been

* Extract from a Salisbury (then Rhodesia) newspaper June 1902.

going down ever since last March when duty was raised. We have piled up an overdraft of £30,000 for cocoa advertising and I can see that the trade in cocoa is a much smaller one than we thought. In addition to this the outlook in chocolate is anything but rosy.'

The situation was still bad in 1902 and the Board thought it prudent to issue £400,000 Debenture shares which were to be under the care of Benjamin Densham.

'Sunday 14 September 1902. Things do indeed look black. We have several cases of moth in the chocolate. I fear we are working on a wrong basis in chocolate and losing money. I also fear trouble with Mr. McQuitty.'

So wrote John Lane as his health continued to deteriorate and he felt he had no alternative but to give up the managing directorship into the hands of McQuitty and Mr Jackson directly after the A G M.

Troubles Mounting...

John Lane's address to shareholders was fully reported in *The Grocer*, 31 March 1906:

'Mr R A McQuitty and Mr H J McClean, who, as you know were managing directors up to 12 December last, I have known and worked with up to three years ago for many years, and I tell you at once they are two of the shrewdest men of business that every came to the City of London. Mr McQuitty I engaged for our advertising department when he was a comparatively young man, and although in carrying out the arrangements with our cocoa and chocolate business he showed want of judgement, he owed his position as managing director of the company to his general business abilities. Mr McClean I engaged when quite a young man to represent us in Ireland and having realised his abilities. I worked him up to the position he held as director and he owes practically everything to me.'

But no sooner had John Lane gone to India, at the Board's request, to organise tea being sent direct from the estates to Russia, America and the British Colonies, than Robert McQuitty and John McClean began a reversal of the firm's founding policy. Up until then it had been the general practice to look after the retailers. In order to diversify, McQuitty and McClean persuaded Benjamin, who had been left with his brother's proxy vote, to open shops around the country, not fully realising the wrath that would be poured on their heads for entering into competition with their own loyal retainers and agents.

The original plan was to öpen five hundred modest, café-type saloons with the sale of packet-tea as a sideline - small places with rents of not more than £60 per annum. However, without the firm hand of John Lane, a kind of insanity infected the project which went ahead without method and with no financial control. One hundred and sixty-four shops were taken with rents running from £160 to £1,000 per annum. Ninety-four premises were equipped at a cost of £178,000. Very splendid shops they were, too, with their colourful tiles, solid mahogany fittings and fine window displays. All these small emporiums have vanished save for one dramatic ceiling covered by a vast painting of *The Old Folks At Home*. This had been papered over and it was not discovered until 1990 when the shop was being redecorated. It is on view in the Aldershot Queens Road Post

Office and Rushmoor Borough Council must be congratulated on giving a £500 grant for conservation.

John Huddleston, McClean's brother-in-law, a former grocer's assistant, had been put in charge of the stock, fittings and redecoration of the new premises. The outlay for these should not have been more than £200 in each case, but in fact on average exceeded £800. Indeed, £10,000 was absorbed by one shop alone. Far from selling only tea, these super shops were to deal in butter, sugar, cheese, sweets and cheap toys. Vast accounts were run up with payments to architects, produce buyers, machinery manufacturers and new staff. Seventeen representatives and a very large number of old employees were summarily dismissed, including Alexander Jackson, as managing director of Densham & Sons, on the trumped-up charge of incompetence. John McClean was promoted to the position.

Meanwhile the new shops were steadily losing money and customers!

Many of these new premises were close to the grocery shops of old and loyal retailers and it was galling for them to see, on opening day, sandwich-board men parading the nearby streets advertising cut-price bargains to lure customers to the Mazawattee super stores. Great bitterness was felt and an extract from a letter to *The Grocer* of 9 September 1905, from Thomas Coote of Surbiton Hill, fully shows the rancour:

> 'I do not like retaliation or boycotting but what I consider would be best and quite justifiable would be for the grocers in each district to combine and agree not to sell Mazawattee tea. They would then be left to possibly a few oil and milk shop agents and their individual efforts at their own shops. This should be done at once. I may add that I am already doing well with my own productions, and what little Mazawattee I may for a while think it wise to stock is finding, and will find, a quiet resting-place on a back, out-of-sight shelf.'

Things were going from bad to worse and an urgent S O S was sent to John Lane, imploring him to return and set matters straight. Although on a health trip he dashed home and, taking in the full horror of the situation, he immediately called an extraordinary general meeting. Learning that the new shops had lost the company £178,426 and hearing of the callous way that former retailers had been pushed aside, the shareholders agreed that shops should be immediately closed and the two

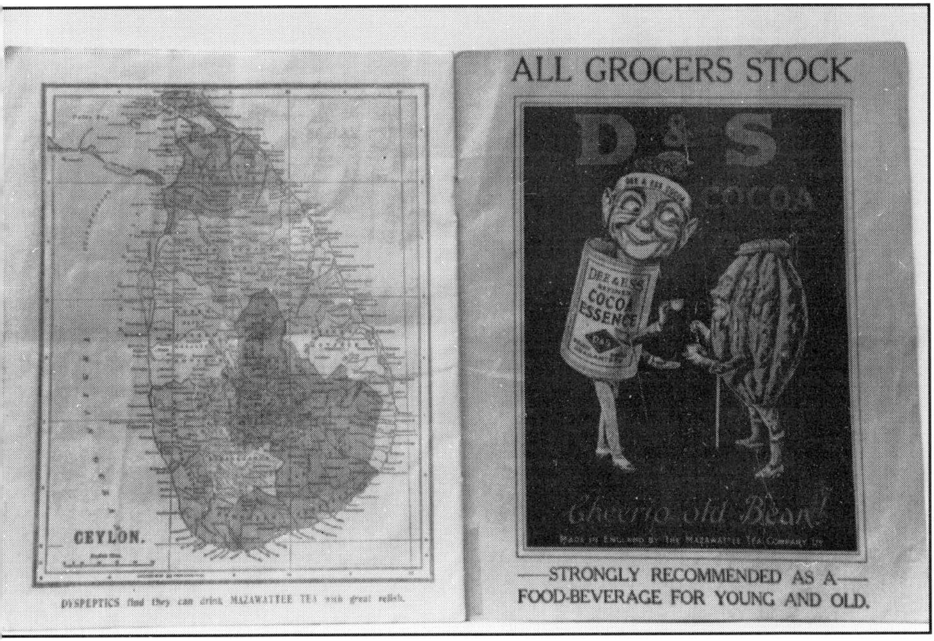

A useful atlas to advertise Mazawattee's D&S (Densham & Sons) cocoa.

A free 'cut out' for children.

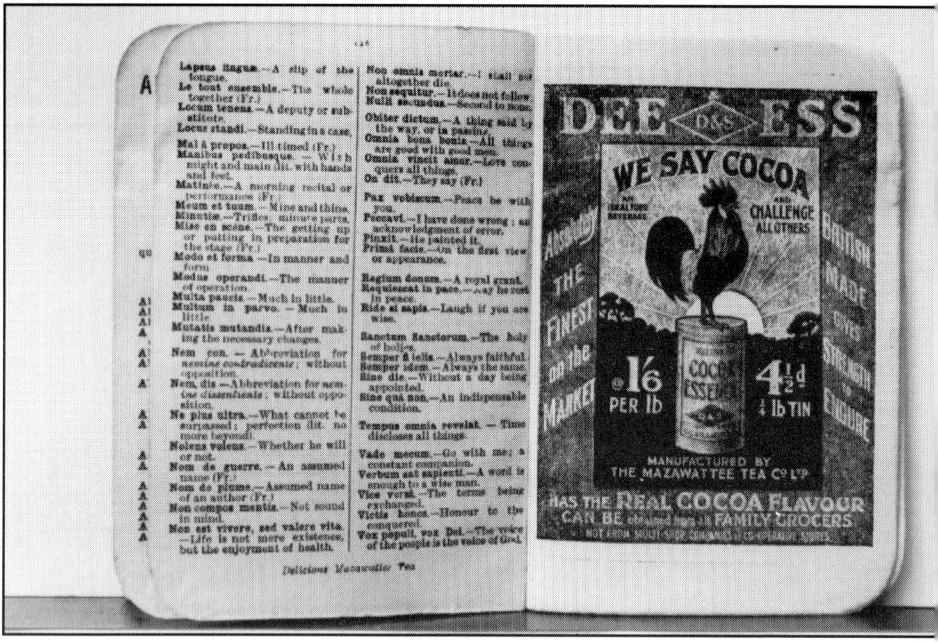

Lapsus linguæ.—A slip of the tongue.
Le tout ensemble.—The whole together (Fr.)
Locum tenens.—A deputy or substitute.
Locus standi.—Standing in a case.
Mal à propos.—Ill timed (Fr.)
Manibus pedibusque.—With might and main (lit. with hands and feet.
Matinée.—A morning recital or performance (Fr.)
Meum et tuum.—Mine and thine.
Minutiæ.—Trifles, minute parts.
Mise en scène.—The getting up or putting in preparation for the stage (Fr.)
Modo et forma.—In manner and form.
Modus operandi.—The manner of operation.
Multa paucis.—Much in little.
Multum in parvo.—Much in little.
Mutatis mutandis.—After making the necessary changes.
Nem. con.—Abbreviation for *nemine contradicente*; without opposition.
Nem. dis.—Abbreviation for *nemine dissentiente*; without opposition.
Ne plus ultra.—What cannot be surpassed; perfection (lit. no more beyond).
Nolens volens.—Whether he will or not.
Nom de guerre.—An assumed name (Fr.)
Nom de plume.—Assumed name of an author (Fr.)
Non compos mentis.—Not sound in mind.
Non est vivere, sed valere vita.—Life is not mere existence, but the enjoyment of health.
Non omnis moriar.—I shall not altogether die.
Non sequitur.—It does not follow.
Nulli secundus.—Second to none.
Obiter dictum.—A thing said by the way, or in passing.
Omnia bona bonis.—All things are good with good men.
Omnia vincit amor.—Love conquers all things.
On dit.—They say (Fr.)
Pax vobiscum.—Peace be with you.
Peccavi.—I have done wrong; an acknowledgment of error.
Pinxit.—He painted it.
Primâ facie.—On the first view or appearance.
Regium donum.—A royal grant.
Requiescat in pace.—May he rest in peace.
Ride si sapis.—Laugh if you are wise.
Sanctum Sanctorum.—The holy of holies.
Semper fidelis.—Always faithful.
Semper idem.—Always the same.
Sine die.—Without a day being appointed.
Sine quâ non.—An indispensable condition.
Tempus omnia revelat.—Time discloses all things.
Vade mecum.—Go with me; a constant companion.
Verbum sat sapienti.—A word is enough to a wise man.
Vice versâ.—The terms being exchanged.
Victis honos.—Honour to the conquered.
Vox populi, vox Dei.—The voice of the people is the voice of God.

Delicious Mazawattee Tea

Mazawattee found 'give-away' dictionaries a good means of advertising.

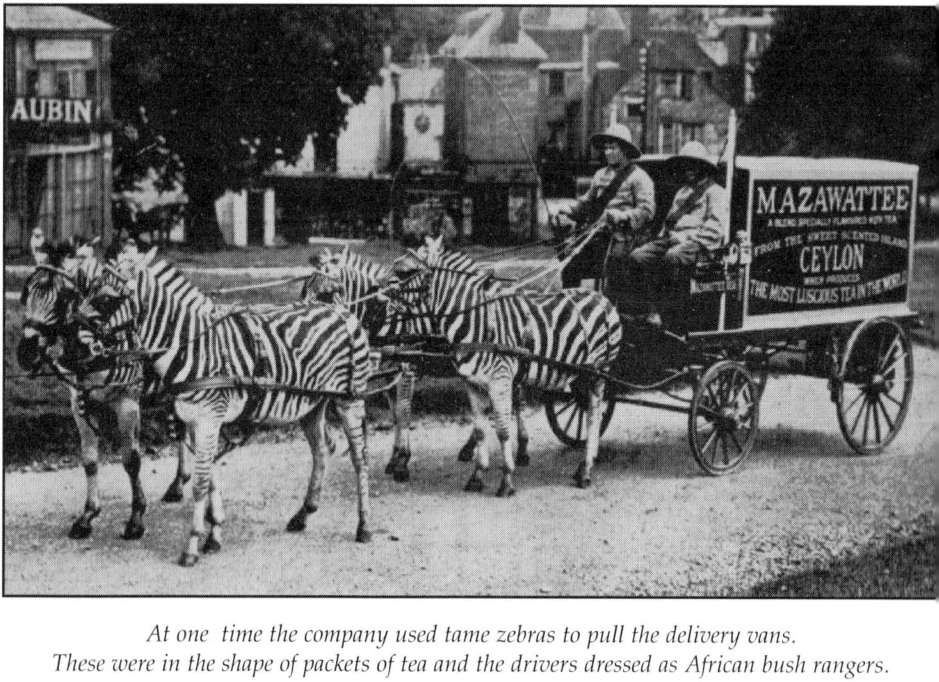

At one time the company used tame zebras to pull the delivery vans.
These were in the shape of packets of tea and the drivers dressed as African bush rangers.

culpable managing directors sacked. Much fury, too, was shown when it was revealed that in September 1905 Robert McQuitty had sold all his Debenture shares, keeping only enough to ensure his remaining a Managing Director. He obviously had no faith in his own policy!

Charges and counter-charges were made, with John McClean and Robert McQuitty vigorously defending their actions. Benjamin Densham had resigned as chairman and disappeared to the country. John Lane was voted back as chairman. When a resolution calling upon John McClean and Robert McQuitty to resign was put to the meeting it was carried 'amid enthusiasm'.

Both gentleman refused to act upon the resolution. John Lane then proposed:

> 'that the meeting regrets that the managing directors have not thought fit to resign, and resolves thereupon that they be forthwith removed from being directors of the company - and that Mr Alexander Jackson and Mr Algernon Charles Oswald be reinstated as directors in the place of the late managing directors, and that Mr Jackson again become managing director.'

The resolution was seconded and carried.

Mazawattee is still remembered in the Dorset 'Knob' factory, Bridport.
This tray dates from 1987. (Courtesy, Raymond Lowe).

Model Bus from the London Transport Museum, December 1983. (Courtesy, John Freeborn).

An advertisement in the Deptford Guide of 1933/34. Horsedrawn wagons, the rail link and the Grand Surrey Canal, with its pleasure boats and barges are featured. The raw materials for the factory would come by water from the Thames docks system.
(Courtesy, Lewisham Historical Society).

A Slow Recovery

The McQuitty and McClean affair caused much heartache and lasting bitterness and the wooing back of the once loyal retailers and agents was a slow business. Indeed, Mazawattee never fully recovered or was able to climb back to the front rank of the tea business.

On 21 May 1906 there was yet more trouble with John McClean. By then he was employed by the Tower Tea Company, and Mazawattee had to file an injunction to prevent their retailers from being poached, and to curtail the use by McClean of information that he had acquired while working at Tower Hill and New Cross. The injunction was granted and it was agreed that the defendant would pay a certain sum.

At the Annual General Meeting of November 1906 some £9,000 had been set aside for special advertising and it was at this time that some of the most attractive and beautifully produced calendars, postcards and booklets were issued. The famous Mazawattee diaries were greatly in demand as were their dictionaries and gazetteers. Artists including A Sheridan Knowles, William Theodore Parkes, Maynard Brown, Louis Wain and Fred Morgan were used to produce designs for tins - enchanting, if occasionally rather sickly, scenes of gallants and their ladies; mothers embracing their daintily dressed little daughters; excellent illustrations of nursery rhymes and fairy tales. These last two categories were planned in series, to encourage customers to collect tins.

The ding-dong dispute of May - June 1906 between the Mazawattee Tea Co and the Maypole Diary Co Ltd, kept both of their names in the headlines. Through the newspapers each threw down the gauntlet in the form of £1,000 to be paid by the loser to the Grocers Benevolent Association. The subject of the challenge was which of the two had actually paid the largest sum ever for tea duty to the customs. There was a certain amount of hitting below the belt, but this lively exchange, with its cut and thrust, was fairly light-hearted publicity for both companies and much enjoyed by the public. *

For the time things were looking up, as shown by an extract from *The Financial World* of 16 March 1907:

> 'No words of appreciation can adequately convey to the directors and management of Mazawattee Tea Co Ltd their admiration which the investing public generally, and their own shareholders in particular, have for the manner in which they have re-

* Full report in *The Grocer* May/June 1906.

established the company to the present gratifying position. Even a year ago most people regarded the situation as almost without hope, but most of us reckoned without our host. We under-estimated the energy and capacity of Mr John Lane Densham and his colleagues on the Board.

This recovery had not been achieved easily for the respect and confidence of retailers had to be earned, once again, and it cost more to win back the trade than it had been to establish it in the first place.'

Just as there seemed to be bright light at the end of the tunnel John Lane suffered another blow. He discovered his brother, Benjamin, had been drinking heavily for years and at times was incapable of transacting business or looking after the interests of the Debenture Shareholders. It was especially upsetting for his scandalous behaviour had come common knowledge in the company and trade. This revelation about Ben was a great shock and John Lane wrote him a brotherly letter, urging him to resign from the Trusteeship of the Debenture Holders.

In a letter of 27 July 1907 he wrote:

'Nothing would have induced me to become co-managing director of a company with you unless you became a teetotaller. The pledge was taken by you in February 1896, and we turned this business into a company the following May.'

No resignation was forthcoming. Agonizing over scandalous stories John Lane wrote to Alexander Jackson, the managing director, in November 1907:

'There can be no shadow of doubt that all the trouble which came upon this business has been through two men of unscrupulous character getting hold of a weak man with a highly respected name, who had been chronically addicted to secret drinking. There are many factors pointing to the probability that these two men got a real hold upon Mr B. Densham. His craven fear of them, as shown in all his letters to them and as evidenced also by his letters to me and by his conduct at all the Board Meetings in invariably siding with them and voting against Mr. Keeble, looks much as if Mr. McQuitty, who knew all about Mr Ben's drinking habits in former years, held this exposure over his head.'

Dorothy and Joseph Densham in the family Daimler, bought in 1906 for £733 10s - licence 5/-.

Under pressure from the Board Benjamin finally resigned.

Like all tea men the members of the Board of Mazawattee were haunted by the ever-present spectre of crushingly heavy duty and co-operated in the forming of an Anti-Tea Duty League. Although the League's efforts knocked a few pence off duty to H M Customs, it was not until 1964 that tea duty was finally abolished.

Again John Lane fought back to rebuild the depleted fortunes of . the company with imaginative advertising and by cultivating new friends and entertaining other companies. The visit of the French grocers seems to have been a special success in this instance.

The Standard of Friday 22 May 1908, reports:

'The delegates of the French Grocers Association who came to London to attend the Anglo-French Congress of Grocers at the Franco-British exhibition spent an enjoyable day as the guests of the Mazawattee Tea Company yesterday. Both the English and French delegates made an early start from the company's offices at Tower Hill, and drove in brakes to the factory at New Cross. There they had a guided tour of all departments and after luncheon, at which Mr John Lane Densham, chairman of the party presided, the whole party was conveyed to Paddington.'

From there a special train, chartered by Mazawattee and brightly decked with the French Tricolour and the Union Jack, took them to Windsor. Permission had been granted for a guided tour of the castle and grounds and 'After tea the return journey was made amid a chorus of congratulations.'

In March 1912 Algernon Oswald died of a brain tumour, having been with the company some 40 years and a tower of strength through troubled days. Joseph Alexander Densham, eldest son of the Chairman was appointed to fill the vacancy. At the age of 31 Joe had 'come up' through the business, travelling widely with his father and had a thorough knowledge of the tea trade.

Time was marching on - Queen Victoria and King Edward VII had died and George V was on the throne. 1914 saw the start of the horrors of the First World War and the City of London became very unsettled.

John Lane's eldest daughter, Evie Tyron, records in her daily diary:

'Wednesday 12 August 1914. They do not seem to know yet to what extent the business may be affected by the war - but they can send

no tea to South Africa, which is a very serious thing for them.'

'*Thursday 20 August 1914*. A police inspector had been to the offices saying they can promise no protection in the case of riots among the bad classes in London and advising their men to join the special constables for their own protection. Joe had already done so.'

'*Friday 21 August 1914*. Father says if Tower Hill were attacked they have decided to leave it and go to New Cross and defend that - they only fear riots come if we have some bad reverses.'

John Lane's three younger sons volunteered for the army while his daughters threw themselves into war work. Stephen Hugh, the baby of the family of fourteen children, died from wounds received in the Battle of Passchendaele. The other two boys survived the carnage of the trenches - Humphrey being decorated for bravery and Patrick living to fight in the Second World War, commanding an A A battery in Malta. Great credit should be given to the older Mazawattee employees, including family relations, of whom Frederick Tryon, John Lane's son-in-law, was outstanding, in their steadfast efforts to keep the tea flowing. Waldronhyrst, the family mansion in Surrey, became a haven for Belgian refugees.

On the Home Front in November 1914 Lloyd George's Budget doubled the tax - putting some 3d on tea and ½d on beer.

At first the Great War had little impact on Mincing Lane and the tea trade in general, but Evie Tryon wrote in her diary:

'*Tuesday 26 Jan. 1915*. Father says they are in a dreadful state in Tower Hill, losing money and don't know what to do - it worries me a good deal.'

'*Friday 5 Feb. 1915*. They have decided at the Board meeting on Monday to wait until the General Meeting to put it to all the shareholders what should be done.'

'*Saturday 6 Mar. 1915*. A wire from Monty Simpson (the Mazawattee Representative) to say fresh duty had been put on tea in South Africa. It will probably mean Father going out to start a factory there.'

"The Sailors Return"
A Mazawattee Tea Calendar of 1923 as an advertisement for T.W. Jarvis in Chadwell Heath.

Meanwhile, German U-boats were stalking allied merchant ships, with the loss of many valuable cargoes, and the Board decided to call a meeting of shareholders to explain the increasing problems.

Deeply troubled, Evie wrote in her diary:
'*Wednesday 14 April 1915*. Father wants to offer £15,000 to the Company to help, if they do not sell short weight tea, as nearly all their competitors do.'

'*Thursday 15 April 1915*. All who have been consulted said Father's money must not be offered, as it was liable to misconstruction. Shareholders and all were practically unanimous in wanting to sell short weight. Father says he will resign the Chairmanship if this happens.'

'*Tuesday 20 April 1915*. A continuation of the Board Meeting - no alteration is to be made at present as to selling short weight on anything.'

'*Thursday 6 May 1915*. They are going to start 3¾ozs packets, with the weight printed on them.'

By now the U-boat menace became much worse and a sad entry in Evie Tryon's diary reads:
'*Saturday 8 May 1915*. News of the sinking of the *Lusitania* by a German submarine - about their worst frightfulness. Hundreds of lives lost - Mr Adams, the Mazawattee representative on board with his second wife, whom he had just married. They (the Company) had a wire "Mrs Adams saved - Mr Adams life uncertain.'

Henry Adams, on honeymoon with his young wife, travelled First Class. The magnificent liner, *Lusitania*, was on its usual run from New York to Liverpool with a full load of passengers. A few miles off the south coast of Ireland it came within torpedo range of U-boat 20, under the command of Kapitänleutnant Walther Schwieger. The missile was fired, striking home between the first and second funnels. Sparks ignited the coal dust and a second terrific explosion proved fatal. The 32,000 ton Cunard liner sank so rapidly - within 20 minutes - the lifeboats and rafts could not be fully loaded, with the result that of the 1,959 passengers 1,198 drowned. In consequence it helped speed up the United States entry into the war.

In an interview given to the *New York Sun* of 25 May 1915, Mrs Adams described her horrific experience. She and Henry donned their life belts and a sailor seated them in one of the collapsible boats. Owing to the ship's list it was lowered unevenly and Mrs Adams was swept away. She managed to cling to an overturned boat for several hours and was eventually rescued by a British naval torpedo craft. The Cunard Steamship Company lists Henry Adam's body being found and identified.

Evie Tryon's diary notes:

> *'Tuesday 21 September 1915*. Day of the Budget Speech. Income tax up 40%. Coffee, cocoa, tea and sugar all taxed more highly.'

This was a bitter blow but Mazawattee was not the only company whose vital commodities were being crippled. In December 1916, following the fall of Mr Asquith, the Food Controller was appointed. As he came to office the price of tea was nearing 3s per lb - quite out of reach of the long-suffering public. However, Lord Devonport ruled that 90 per cent of all imported tea was still not classified as a food and had been included in the list of luxury drinks and foodstuffs by the Imports Restriction Committee. Therefore, only some 6,000 tons a month were imported - instead of the 15,000 tons before the war. Very long queues, especially for tea and margarine, besides much grumbling from the housewives, brought the Ministry to its senses and merchant ships were dispatched and fresh contracts made with India and Ceylon, to buy their entire crops of tea. From autumn 1917 the Ministry became the sole importer of tea. By 1918 90 percent was price controlled and licences issued to dealers and merchants according to their sales over the datum period. Auctions at Mincing Lane were virtually phased out as tea had become National Control tea, pegged to a retail price of 2s 8d.

Evie Tryon's diary reads:

> *'Saturday 13 April 1918*. Rationing has begun all over England. We get 7 coupons each, worth 5d each - 3 for the butcher and 1 for other sorts.'

For tea, the housewife had to register with her local shop where the retailer had an allowance of 2oz per customer.

'*Friday 24 May 1918.* Some new Government order has come out and Fred will have to be away next week to try to get as many grocers to register with Mazawattee as possible before June 1st. He is very worried.'

'*Saturday 1 June 1918.* Fred got home very anxious, I can see, about the future. Tea orders are altered - the date extended.'

Troubles piled high for the company and with the intention of starting a factory in Port Elizabeth John Lane and his wife travelled out to South Africa. His health was failing, and, tortured with stomach pains and nerves the blow of his son's death was a shock from which he never recovered. He contracted para-typhoid and died at the house of his married daughter, Dorothy Durell, on 13 February 1918. With his death went one of the company's greatest assets.

THE AUSTRALIAN CRICKETERS

Can play with anybody the National Game, and enjoy with everybody the National Tea—Delicious MAZAWATTEE.

The Tea Interval at Lords Cricket Ground.

Changes...

Alexander Jackson, a small stocky man, bristling with energy, succeeded John Lane Densham to become a good and wise chairman. He had joined Mazawattee as a tea taster and it was he, in 1891, who made the famous bid of £25 10s per pound for the 'Gartmore Golden Tips'. He steered Mazawattee through the troubled war years, slumps, strikes and heavy taxes of the period. Many of the most amusing advertisements were produced under his chairmanship. One way of charming money out of the public pocket was by having delivery vans pulled by teams of four zebras. Photocards were given to the shops in advance, showing the harnessed animals with their sola-topeed and khaki clad African drivers. The back of each card reads:

> 'The famous Mazawattee Team of Zebras will visit here today. Look out for them and do not miss seeing these marvellous animals. It is well known that the zebra is one of the most difficult animals to train. These have been trained from birth. It can therefore be seen what a great difficulty there must have been in training them to run in harness. Mazawattee Tea can be obtained from all family grocers, full weight without wrappers at 1/6, 1/8, 1/10, 2/-, 2/6, 3/-, 3/4 per pound.'

This interesting spectacle must have caused traffic jams and been a source of delight to goggle-eyed pedestrians.

After the First World War there were bad times for the country and the Empire Tea Growers' Association were pushing the "Buy British" campaign. The great British Empire Exhibition at Wembley, 1924, appealed to the public to support British goods. Mazawattee enthusiastically advertised that all their products were handled only by British workpeople. It was also proud to boast: 'Teas from the choicest gardens of India and Ceylon - Empire grown throughout and brought by Empire ships - are dealt with by a British firm employing British labour.'

By now *The Old Folks At Home* advertisement had become slightly modernised - so losing much of its early charm. The horse-drawn vans were replaced by motorised ones in the shape of tea packets with a shining imitation silver tea-pot on the roof. Out of the spout exuded exhaust - supposedly to represent steam.

In 1933 Alexander Jackson died at his home in Dulwich and Joseph Alexander Densham became chairman. These were the lean years with business troubles mounting.

DELICIOUS MAZAWATTEE TEAS.

"Little Nell"
A give-away leaflet for Geo. E. Paulin, coffee and tea dealer of Hoddesdon, Herts.

The Gathering Twilight...

In 1933, at the age of 17, Costin Lane Densham joined the company and his memories vividly portray the final days of the once great Mazawattee Tea Empire.

'I was put to work in the so-called 'clearing'department under Mr Geary. Bowler-hatted and with everyone calling me Mister Costin, all seemed set for a rosy future. My salary was £1 a week, the senior tea boy received 30/- and Mr Brooker, who was well over 90, £2. He would go quite frantic when we mischievous tea boys stuck weights under his scales, so throwing out his calculations! I do remember a tea chest being opened and out slid a cobra. It was jolly hungry after the three weeks trip from Assam!

'Looking back to an age when education was 'scrappy' to say the least, I am amazed at how well 'un-educated' people wrote, even the youngest tea boy could write legibly and well. Any mistake was mercilessly jeered and poor handwriting much frowned upon. Likewise, with the difficulties of weights and measures and invoicing, most could do quite complicated sums, including multiplying $^3/_4$ds in their heads. The 3 Rs were perhaps better taught in those days?

Upstairs in the Clearing Department and invoicing room steel pens were always used - the Pickwick, the Owl and the Waverley nibs being popular. Blotting paper was much in evidence and ink powder, mostly Stephens, copiously mixed. Fountain pens were not allowed, except in the Sale room. My own writing was poor, but improved under the jeering, and eventually got, if not up to standard, passable. It is not easy to write on a 2oz. sample with no support for your right hand, especially when you might have to get on as much as "30c Bogourabtakawa Fannings" and then clearly mark the price. The whole process of doing up small samples (with grease proof paper inside) was quite an art in itself. You could throw a good one hard on the floor and tread on it and the paper would not come undone. No glue was used - it was simply paper folding. Perhaps some 20 or 30 of these had to be made into a big parcel for posting. You soon got to know how much paper and string to tear and cut off to save wastage.

Blending, too, was an art, using two 'funnelled' pieces of paper and mixing up to 12 teas without dropping any on the floor. Real sleight of hand had to be used, because if one of your papers

Mazawattee Ford delivery van used in the 1930s. The exhaust came out of the tea-pot's spout.

The Rev. Costin Lane Densham,
1916-1987.
The last generation of the Denshams to work
for Mazawattee Tea.

Trade calendar of 1930 for R&C Robertson,
Lerwick, Shetland.

Mazawattee Chocolates now in cardboard boxes.
(Courtesy, Antony Hebdon)

buckled you lost the lot and that was the ultimate disgrace."

Costin Densham describes a typical working day:
'I would leave Wallington on the 8.05 each morning and travel by Southern Railway. The season ticket (3rd Class, of course) was £3 18s. 9d. per quarter. Gradually one got used to the routine. May, our sales lady, put on the enormous kettles every morning, each holding enough water for 60 cups of tea and each equipped with a whistle. We worked like beavers, setting out the 300 odd rows of tea tins - weighing up the amount to be put in each sampling pot - filling up - starting the stop watches on the wall, which pinged in exactly 6 minutes. We then turned the liquor into the testing bowls and dropped the leaves into the upturned lids. It was amazing how one's right arm and hand developed to carry and tip the huge kettles. A few scalds and soaked trousers soon disciplined you! Then Tommy Covel and Lee Hawkins or Mr Whitehill would appear and tasting would commence. Armed with the catalogue we youngsters would accompany them, putting down their 'valuations' in code. These codes were great fun, and we always tried to 'break' our rivals efforts, so that the buyers could see what other firms were prepared to bid. Dutifully we noted the tasters' remarks with 'Good liquor' or 'Dusty but good flavour' and the price. We would take a sip ourselves and then expertly spit the stuff out into the spittoons that poor May had to empty and wash in disinfectant, ready for the next day. A 'likely' buy would have milk added as a double check.
'At about 11 a.m. with some 300 or 350 teas behind you, the Sale Rooms in Mincing Lane opened, and the buyers departed thither. Mondays and Wednesdays were Indian days, Tuesday Ceylon and Thursday Sumatra, Java and China.
'From 11 a.m. until about 3.30 p.m. saleroom boys had to shuffle between saleroom and office, bringing back catalogues, entering up and sending off for big samples of the teas that had been purchased, ready to be posted off to loose tea buyers that evening. At first the Auction Room sounded like bedlam, but one soon got used to the grunts and shouts and began to understand them. Gradually the day passed, but often, especially during the New Season Sales it was 7.30 p.m. sometimes 9.00 p.m. before we had finished. We got 1/- 'tea money' on those occasions. Overtime was unheard of but nobody grumbled, we just set to and made our

own fun having spent tea money on beer and sandwiches. In the area were many small cafes and pubs with dining rooms where you could get a three course meal for as little 1/2d. There was the Tiger Inn at Tower Hill which served beautiful French bread, butter and cheese. That, and ¹/₂ a pint of bitter cost you 11d! The story that tea tasters don't drink or smoke is largely fabrication.

'When Chairman, my Father had made by a special firm, two full sized working models for advertising purposes. One was a Town Crier who had a speaker in his stomach - a 9 inch record. As he rang his bell he proclaimed "Oyez. Oyez. It is decreed that all loyal subjects should drink Mazawattee tea etc. etc". At an exhibition at the Crystal Palace, some wit from Brooke Bond sabotaged him, and, when switched on, he began to bellow "The Stein Song.'

Their other dramatic advertisement was a full sized *Old Folks* where Granny poured from tea pot to cup, drank deeply and nodded her head. The liquid flowed back via a pipe from the cup handle - down a rubber tube hidden in her sleeve and returned to the tea pot. At an exhibition at Portsmouth the mechanism went wrong, and there she sat, pouring tea and then throwing it over her left shoulder at the assembled spectators. Nobody could get near her until she ran dry.

'Our 'relief'day was Saturday, when all the travellers came up in the morning, bringing the latest dirty jokes and gossip and trying to 'fiddle' certain teas for their special customers.

'As I got used to it all I began to sense the crisis situation that was developing. Sales were not increasing. The Ordinary Dividend dropped to 5% from a steady 15% and we had no 1/4d packet, as did our rivals, the Co-op and Typhoo. The times were poor, unemployment was rife. It was difficult to sell tea, especially in the depressed areas where grocers were having to break open even 1/4lb packets and sell small 'screws' of tea to the poorer families. Part of New Cross was let to J Stones & Co, the foundry people, and we introduced 'divi' stamps, but it was already too late. Many of our old customers took longer and longer to pay and we could do nothing but accommodate. The last thing before the war was the production of "gas tight" tins, of which every grocer was asked to keep a month's supply. Under the conditions of 1939 this was handled quickly and efficiently. As soon as war broke out all firms were allotted a quota, based on average yearly sales. Then everything froze. The markets ceased, rationing was fairly quickly introduced, so the travellers could no longer sell tea. All luxury trading stopped and under rationing tea sold itself so that Mazawattee was able to make a small profit.

'The younger staff members went into the forces and the company was in the hands of the valiant old guard.

'I shall never forget the sight of the Tower Hill offices after the bombing, one night in 1940. Stairs with polished brass treads I had galloped up so often; the old hydraulic lift; the gallery which overlooked the sale room, each with their sad and hilariously happy memories, lay in quite miserable ruin. I just remember seeing the white back of one of the directors' urinals, still sticking to the wall of the bonded warehouse next door.

'Not long after this the New Cross works were nearly obliterated - the 100 ton fly wheel of the Crossley gas engine exploded on being hit and it is alleged, that part of a spoke was picked up in Sydenham. The destruction of Tower Hill and New Cross gave my father the opportunity of regenerating his friendship with Mr Edward Gray of Brooke Bond, who did all our packing for the duration. The company took offices from Furness, Withy and Co in Leadenhall Street, but it was now just a 'puppet' concern, staffed by brave men who stood days and nights of fire watching, air raids, V1 flying bombs and V2 rockets with complete equanimity.

'After having battled through the war years my Father became bedridden and lost all interest in the firm, for the men he had grown up with, knew and trusted, had died. In the tea world a man's word was his bond. Thousands of pounds changed hands at the mere lift of a finger. Good solid British values, I suppose one must say. Edwardian England represented the end of an age. Looking back at these men I can only say "May the Old Folks be at Home!"

The Revd Costin Lane Densham's memories of a once great company bring to life an epoch never to return.

Robert McGreivy has many stories concerning his years with the Mazawattee Tea Company at New Cross during the country-wide depression of those pre-war days. He recalls this unhappy era:

"In the thirties, a new manager was brought in from J Lyons, to reorganise the sweetmaking, cocoa and chocolate side. This entailed many changes of layout and the New Building was earmarked for a venture into seaside rock manufacture. The coffee extract plant on the top floor was moved over to the empty building next to the boiler house which had previously been used for storing paper cartons and sacks of coffee. The coffee extract was again put on the top floor whilst Lorimer Marshall occupied the ground and first floor. All this took a couple of months before everything was connected up and production resumed. Then the seaside rock had to be put into swing, but it seemed to we ordinary folk a forlorn hope to compete against the established trade. And so this proved and to many of us it was the real cause of the demise of Samuel Allen & Co, Densham & Sons, D & S Cocoa and all the subsidiary companies, and worst of all, so many lost jobs.

'In 1936 the confectionery side was closed down. I remember that the whole of the engineering staff was sent to the West Wing to dismantle the boiling pans and other pieces of equipment ready for scrap. Also, over the following weeks, the cocoa, chocolate and toffee processing plants were all scrapped - no chance of a competitor getting hold of some cheap machinery! By this time war was looming and, as the West Wing was empty J Stone & Co were housed to make fire bombs, I helped to install some of their equipment before I left to join the Royal Navy, serving in D.E.M.S. for the duration.'

Returning from the war, in 1945, Robert McGreivy describes the sad state in which he found the once magnificent New Cross Factory.

'J Stone & Co had moved out of the West Wing and this had been taken over by the scrap metal merchants, J & J Maybanks. It was a shame to see the once proud main entrance being cluttered up with rag and bone men and their one horse traps loaded with bits of lead piping, brass taps etc, 'rescued' from the bombed houses and local buildings.'

In 1941, 17 years old, Sylvia Lambert joined the Traffic Department at New Cross as a shorthand typist where, under the Essential Works Order, she stayed for 5 years. Happy years too, in spite of the Blitz. Her reminscences give a vivid picture of those years with Mazawattee.

'I started working at New Cross in the October after it had been bombed the previous spring, so I never knew the factory as it had been.

'The general office roof had been replaced with tarpaulin and everywhere was dirty and very cold. I remember we wore our topcoats in the winter and a large cast-iron stove in the middle of the room was a focal point for lunch time breaks and to defrost. In the summer, of course we could sit by the canal, which was very pleasant, until the sirens went.

'In a smaller room to one side Mr Blackmore and his staff handled all factory wages and PAYE and there was a steady stream of young ladies from the workshops with their queries and grievances and ready for a fight.

'In another corner a dear little old man by the name of Veness sat designing labels and tea packets and I had the task of trying to decipher his dreadful writing before typing the orders for the printers. Sometimes he would send me down to the Letterpress at the end of the factory. This had been almost completely destroyed and on opening the great doors one just walked into the open air where large white stone blocks lay scattered on the ground like a Greek ruin.

'There was also the Toolshop and Tinprinting shop, coffee roasting and blending rooms, tea blending and packing department and right at the very end of the factory was the Lorimer-Marshall area, producing essences, talcum powder, and among a host of other things a concoction called 'Ru Mari', a rheumatic cure of which we seemed to sell a great deal. They also made a beef extract and the whole district knew when that was being processed.

'The Clock tower was over the main entrance. One side was the weighbridge office, and here we clocked on and off. Here also, once a week Bill Cornish ran a little shop where we could buy our tea and sweet ration. In a room under the clock I remember seeing a collection of Mazawattee tins and also a large painting of the old lady and little girl.'

In April 1948 the situation for the company was still far from rosy. A minimum payment of £450.00 per annum being guaranteed plus commission and out-of-pocket expenses, to their travellers, seemed rather ungenerous - but times were hard and wages low.

Schedule of Commission Rates
Mazawattee Tea
Quality   3/4d   3/8d   4/2d
        Per lb   ½d   ¾d   1d

Mazawattee Coffee
        4/- per 100 lbs

Teas from Densham & Sons Ltd
        Blended Tea and Original Teas, one third of net
        profit on stated valuations

Coffee from Densham & Sons Ltd
        4/- per 100 lbs

Coffee Extract
        5%

Lorimer - Marshall Goods
        5%

Edwin Ebsworth, a senior salesman displays a phial of the Golden Tips.
(Courtesy, Aldershot Star).

*A ceiling, covered by a huge picture of "The Old Folks At Home",
in the sub Post Office in Queens Road, Aldershot Hants.
(Courtesy, Richard Densham).*

*A long term contract ensured that every railway station in the British Isles displayed
Mazawattee Tea signs. This is part of the Ironbridge Museum complex.
(Courtesy, Henry Jeffery)*

*Mazawattee Tea is still remembered in South Africa.
The name has again become popular since Nelson Mandela
used Mazawattee granny spectacles as part of his disguise.
A new reproduction tin.*

Nearing the End

Costin Densham never returned to Mazawattee after the war but his younger brother, David, became acting secretary for a short while after the death of W T (Billy) Rest. He was the last of the Denshams to serve the company. The old guard was passing into the shadows as in 1952 Frederick Jackson and Ronald Law retired, having given many years to the tea trade. Joseph Densham retired in 1953 after 50 years with Mazawattee. He died in 1960. It seemed that nothing now could save the company. It passed rather rapidly through the hands of Neville Allan-Smith, who sold the New Cross site for a sum large enough to make a profit to The Excelsior Biscuit Company. This was a subsidiary of the wholesalers, Burton, Son & Sanders Ltd. Burtons was a publicly quoted company, specialising in the manufacture of prepared materials for the bakery trade, but also acting as a wholesale grocer from its branches in Ipswich, Norwich and Colchester. The company was thriving up to 1939 and this continued up to the end of sugar rationing in 1954. During that period, the biggest problem was that of obtaining new raw materials, and all sorts of weird methods were found of importing sugar added to fat, or as an ingredient in 'dry mincemeat'. Burtons bought several companies at this time purely because they had large allocations of sugar, such as Barrett & Pomeroy and Ambrose, both fairly large bakers in the London area. Rather later, they bought the Excelsior Biscuit Company, who had an enormous bakery with a huge allocation of rationed products.

David Lingham, who was a branch manager for Burton, Son & Sanders remembers:

> 'It is my impression that Mazawattee came into the fold at this time, probably as a subsidiary of Excelsior. However, it might have been bought at that time as a tax-loss company. I seem to remember that we did sell a limited amount of Mazawattee packet tea. My next recollection must come from about 1960, when Keith Stainton, our chairman at the time, sent a confidential letter to all branch managers. I was in charge of our Belfast branch at that time, and I was requested to track down one or two named shareholders in Mazawattee, so that we could obtain their shares in order to take advantage of accumulated tax losses. This was not straight-forward, either, because they were old, and at least one of mine was

ga-ga! However, I managed to track down financial advisers in each case.'

For a while Mazawattee was packed by one of the big tea companies, and the Quick Brew Tea could be bought in Woolworths and similar stores. Its London address was then 50 Thomas Road, London E 14 and the business was under E A Heckford, Director and Secretary. By then the tea had lost its former magnificent quality and finally was no longer obtainable.

In the late 1960s an experimental survey was tried in one of the northern areas to see if the trade mark meant anything to the present generation of housewives and might be worth reviving. The result proved negative.

Is this the end of the story? Not quite!

The Mazawattee Tea vaults, deep in the heart of Tower Hill, have been excavated and turned into small shops and restaurants, while the Museum of London has put on a Pageant of History there. On the present wave of nostalgia, South Africa - once its biggest overseas customer - is reproducing attractive Mazawattee tins. Spain has just launched packets of tea featuring *The Old Folks At Home*. Indeed, the *Old Folks* post cards are now best sellers in the Robert Opie Collection of advertising material in Gloucester. Children are snapping up a model Golden Arrow double decker bus, advertising Mazawattee as *British and Best!* Like the Phoenix could the Granny and Little Girl rise from the ashes of Tower Hill and New Cross? Maybe Corgi Toys were prophetic when they launched a splendid die-cast model tram. Across the side, on a green background, a large message proclaims

"Drink Mazawattee Tea"

The Mazawattee New Cross Complex, 1933.

The Mazawattee Head Office destroyed by fire bombs in 1940.

Make Tea The Mazawattee Way

Follow these simple rules to ensure the perfect cup of tea.

1　Always use freshly drawn, cold water in the kettle. Water that has boiled already has had the oxygen bubbled out of it.

2　Buy good quality tea and don't be afraid to experiment to make your own blend by mixing different loose leaf teas.

3　When the kettle is near boiling point heat the tea pot with some of the hot water - swirl it around before emptying the contents away.

4　Always take the heated pot to the kettle and, just before it boils, and the loose leaf tea, or bags, to the pot. A rough guide is to measure one teaspoon per person and one for the pot.

5　Immediately the water boils pour it on the leaves.

6　Slip a tea cosy over the pot and allow to draw. Usually small leaf tea needs to stand for three minutes and the larger leaves for six minutes.

7　When pouring the golden liquid into the cups be sure to use a tea strainer.

The Mazawattee people decided that the most delicious brews were made in homely, brown earthenware, or porcelain pots. Nowadays teapots with internal holders can ensure that all the leaves are lifted out, after the tea has drawn. Some connoisseurs consider that if the leaves are left to stew in the pot the taste becomes bitter. Here lies the advantage of tea bags as they can be easily ejected. In 1948 an American tea bag machine was installed in the New Cross factory and, when the Company went out of business in 1952, the machine was transferred to the Aldgate factory of Brooke Bond Tea. However, the Mazawattee tasters thought it did not make such a good drink. There was also the possibility that the bags might have been bleached to enhance their appearance. In respect of which, never put a tea pot in a dish washer as the strong, cleansing chemicals might linger and flavour the tea.

Whether to Add Milk And Sugar

This is a personal choice but adding sugar does affect the taste buds so that the full flavour of the tea is not experienced. Milk certainly enhances some strong teas and should be put in the cup first. Added to the tea there is a possibility of greasy globules floating on the surface, unless the milk is absolutely fresh. The more delicately flavoured brews are often spoilt by the addition of milk - though a slice of lemon can greatly add to the piquancy.

Follow these rules and you will never fail to make a delicious pot of tea - the Mazawattee way.